This way to the exit ...

Janet Kenny

© 2012, Janet Kenny. All Rights Reserved. This material may not be reproduced in any form, published, reprinted, recorded, performed, broadcast, rewritten or redistributed without explicit permission of Janet Kenny. All such actions are strictly prohibited under law. ISBN-13: 978-0615615936 ISBN-10: 0615615937

White Violet Press
1840 West 220th Street Suite 300
Torrance, California 90501

To Music

Acknowledgments

Poems in this collection have been published as follows:

The Barefoot Muse: Seen From Above.
The Chimaera: Daft; Hushabye; Last Dance; Out There.
Del Sol Review: Du.
Filled with Breath: 30 sonnets by 30 poets (*Exot Books*):
    To Franz Schubert
The Flea: Articulated; Powerless; Sightlines; Takeoff.
14 x 14: Old Apple.
The Guardian: My Father's Eyes.
The Hyper Texts: Du; My Father's Eyes; To a Dying Rat.
Iambs & Trochees: Eternal Hope.
Lavender Review: Butterflies.
The Raintown Review: Antal Szalai's Gypsy Band in an
    Australian Country Town; Eternal Hope; 'No'.
Shit Creek Review: Mangoes.
Soundzine: Out Loud.
The Spectator: To a Dying Rat.
Susquehanna Quarterly: To a Dying Rat.
Umbrella: Rain from a Blue Sky

Contents

Takeoff 9
War 13
My Father's Eyes 14
Bicycle 15
Mangoes 19
In the Wet 20
Old Apple 22
Moonlight as a Woodcut 23
Orang-utan 24
Out There 25
Hushabye 26
Du 31
Along the Darkening Shore 32
'No' 34
Last Dance 35
Moving Right Along 36
Daft 39
Articulated 40
Eternal Hope 42
Sightlines 44
Rain from a Blue Sky 45
The Pigeons in the Square 46
To Franz Schubert (1797–1828) 47

Antal Szalai's Gypsy Band in an Australian Country Town 48
Celebrity Recital 50
Out Loud 55
To a Dying Rat 56
Despite 57
Seen From Above 61
Powerless 62
Butterflies 63
About the Author 64

facing the music

Takeoff

Fasten your seat belt, close your eyes, ignore
the musical panic caused by what you hear,
count very slowly as the engines roar,
clutch at the arm rest as the time draws near
for that unstable moment as the vast
body turns round and moves towards the spot
where it will snarl and tear along so fast
that you relive your past, then like a shot,
up, bumping through the cloud towards the sun,
breaking the hold of earth with jolts till high,
suddenly freedom floats you through the spun
wisps Leonardo dreamed of in a sky
he never saw except inside his brain.
You are his eyes, through you he lives again.

reaching for the door handle

War

I recall a beach with barbed wire rolled
below the dunes to fence off iron sand.
Together with my family who strolled
beyond the barbed wire, I tried to understand
why it was dangerous enough to arm
this wilderness, but safe enough for us
to play in front of pill boxes, no harm
expected, so no need to make a fuss.
A wrecked ship lay agape and gouged the beach.
Dark torrents rushed around its rusty hulk,
and hostile gulls blew fast with warning screech
while workmen carted off the iron bulk.
And if the Japanese came, who were they?
So, self-absorbed, we kept on with our play.

My Father's Eyes

So blue, my father's eyes out of the river;
he swam too long, I held my frightened breath
sure that some weed or log had caused his death.
Then with a rush the water would deliver
his face, triumphant at my lack of faith.
Proud of his power to frighten me. I never
believed he would survive. He seemed forever
imprisoned in some crevice underneath.
To venture in that dark and rushing pool
was more than I could bear. I chose to swim
in sunlit shallows where cicadas' prattle
and softly dipping willows made a cool,
consoling summer refuge. Nothing grim
could lurk, or rise intent to smirk and startle.

Bicycle

bicycle lifts me quietly
wheelwoman speeds
lightly
no bird ceases song
when my bicycle
wheels along
no flower lost scent
where my bicycle
went
past bright weeds, no air
fouls when bicycle
is there
spokes spin over metal
momentum spurred
by pedal
elegant machine
so clean nobody knows
you've been.

natural curiosity

Mangoes

As mangoes bash the iron shed
and moonlight floods the grizzled lawn
I think of what I should have said
and toss in bed until the dawn.

Masked lapwings passing overhead
repeat their old nocturnal pain,
kekekeke, a song of dread,
the sun has gone away again.

I talk with all my loving dead,
who tell me they have always known
that light and darkness have misled
the living who are not alone.

Hear fruit-bats screech as overfed
they thunder heavy mangoes down.
A drunk, percussive aliped,
a Nosferatu on the town.

The crows are up. My eyes instead
shut down to miss the morning sun.
The bats, the lapwings, now have fled
my friends leave with them, one by one.

In the Wet

(Queensland plaint)

Monsoon is falling down the coast
and driving oxygen away.
High fans rotate as bodies splay
in damp display like soggy toast.

Grass growing visibly invites
the roar of motor-mower now,
since fear of neighbours makes a row
more deafening than monsoon fights.

Maintaining standards in the heat
has always been the final test
that none dares fail, each does the best
they can, though many find defeat.

The rain falls upwards from the ground
as well as down; which way is moot.
Unless it's down, they don the boot
and angry motors scream and pound.

The grass is graceful, fungus strewn,
with toxic mushrooms sprung like toads
around the houses, by the roads,
a gift that grows beneath the moon.

They mow them flat and spray them far
and few, until they reappear,
more numerous and twice as queer,
that's how monsoonal fungi are.

Monsoon is falling down the coast
and Celtic humans gasp and sweat,
inelegant, not beaten yet;
the victors those who mow the most.

Old Apple

I picked an apple from a twisted tree
because its green-gold skin was dull and rough.
Half pear, half apple, from a history
when orchards grew less calculated stuff.

The skin seemed almost wooden when I bit,
but soda or champagne erupted, fresh
as fountains in a forest. I had hit
on Eve's defiant, psychotropic mesh.

These apples lurk abandoned behind walls
too broken and moss-covered to invite
commercial growers. There an orchard sprawls
neglected, dark and sinful as the night.

Wild offspring of the rose and bramble bear
the chemistry of love and harsh despair.

Moonlight as a Woodcut

Mice, lit by moonlight, stand too tall,
with shadow legs like barley stalks
to tantalise the roving fox
and signal to the watchful owl.

Clouds dim the moon's bright disc so night
can hide the scuttling creatures worn
by a forensic hunters' moon
that magnifies the desperate.

Tiger burning in the black
Blake made to drive us mad with awe,
the moon will show us where you are
although night's forest is so thick.

Cool, impartial goddess, shine
on us with equal empathy.
Flood sheets of light on ground and sky,
embalm us with your silver stain.

Orang-utan

If my arms were gangly like theirs, I'd swing in the canopy,
lope in elliptical attitudes, changing my shape,
study and try to avoid unavoidable entropy,
learn about edible fruits from a scholarly ape.
I'd leap in arboreal loops through the tangled immensity
and dangle through chlorophyll rays in a luminous sky
Below me the forest would glow with a jade-like intensity;
I'd dance over darkness, unfurl with the orchids and fly.

Out There

One moment light, then dark—no power.
The suburb stopped in sullen shock,
without a warning, for a block
all motors died for half an hour.
Twittering heedless through the trees,
two small marauding ringtail possums
cheerfully sought for shoots and blossoms
unaware of our unease.
Little marsupials, monkey-tailed,
hooked on branches and extended
hands for flowers which were intended
for such as these, then up they sailed
as though no gravity existed;
over canopies they skittered,
barely touching as they littered
poo and petals till they misted
into darkness where they vanished,
leaving me to wait for light
and when it came, too harsh, too bright,
I longed for what my world had banished.

Hushabye

In the silence of the night lie all that's good and all that's bad.
A meditation or a fight, a fright that drives a sleeper mad.
And if I die before I wake, forgive the unobserved mistake.

No lie can make the mountains quake. Beneath the sky our houses shake.
The seeker after truth will fall and, bruised and shaken, hide in shame.
Tomorrow he will not recall the fall, but do it all again.

The child who wakes as horrid crone will not have grown inside her head,
But spend her nursery days alone and die forgotten in her bed.

There's no escape from minutes marked in darkness waiting for the light.
Before your eyes your life will flash, slow-motion in a silent night.

A silent night where dark things skulk behind the towering wardrobe's bulk.
Beneath the bed a catafalque, a silken spread for scolds to sulk.
God bless the skull that's got his own, a bunch of ribs, a finger bone.

Around the palace thorns have grown and bandits hanker for the throne.
A prince will come without a face, a cutlass, riding breeks, and lace.
He seeks a mask to fill the space, but leaves expelled by dogs and mace.

Something important seems to lurk between the hours of sleep
   and work.
And yet it lingers in the murk, a Cheshire cat without a smirk.

In the silence of the night we lie awaiting ancient spite.
God bless the child who strikes a spark, and fans its glow to
   light the dark.
The doors are armed, the windows locked, no one is harmed, no
   subject shocked.
Trees drum the roof with time to kill. Broad daylight finds us
   lying still.

the importance of love

Du

A wisp of old woman,
curved like a scythe,
tottered to me as she
fussed her shopping,
her walking stick hooked
on her chopstick wrist.

She spoke to me then
in a dried-leaf voice.
Inaudible there
in that busy street,
swept by rude gales
from passing trucks.

I leaned closer to hear:
Mein eyes not gut.
Time for bus, ven comes it?
'Which bus do you want?'

She smiled, shook her head
then sang to herself
and somebody else,
in—not German. Yiddish?
'Which bus?'
She leaned towards me,
her tiny claw reached
to stroke my face.
Du, she said.

Du.

Along the Darkening Shore

Under the fire-ball evening sky the sea
gentled around my toes. The sand was rose
and golden as the furtive tide encroached
and crept inshore. Here was the verb 'to be'.
'To do' was walking lengthwise through the wash
as tribal lorikeets massed high in trees
that fringed the beach for miles. Cicadas beat
their ground-bass brightly for the silver stream
of parrot-screech and gossip in their roost.

'Shhh', said the water, 'listen to the world.
Nothing is what it was. It only seems
the same. Walk through my shallows. There's no cost
but loss of wanting. You are growing old
yet nothing that you value will be lost.
Look at that woman, older than you, yet she
landed a stingray on the beach. She knew
what was beneath my gentle velvet face.
Nothing is harmless. Neither she nor you.
Both of you may bring death close to this place.
Did you observe the woman up the beach?
Shrieking that nothing was familiar. "Where?
Where am I now?" she screamed but no-one spoke.
Near her a man stood motionless and stared
at the horizon, paying her no heed.
She crumpled, sobbing. He refused to look.'
Dark in the bat-filled sky a gliding kite
searched for bewildered wanderers in the night.

Water and I moved miles along the edge
Water came in—and I walked still along
paddling and wading in deceptive calm
warmed by the day's remembered tropic sun.
Even the roosting lorikeets were hushed.
'Water, I feel respect but do not trust
water nor fire nor air. I come from dust'.

'No'

Old Mark cries 'No' and 'No' again.
His protest flies across the park.
It enters houses. 'No' his pain
cannot be stopped from dawn to dark.
'No, No' each moment is his first
awareness that he's hit the wall.
What was is gone. His heart must burst
each moment that he grasps it all.
The twilight home that holds his hell
is well endowed, of good repute.
The inmates in each private cell
cry 'No' although their cries are mute.
Children stop their play to ask
Why does the man keep shouting 'No'?
Their mothers don the adult mask
and maximise the radio.

Last Dance

Old lovers promenade the beach,
bare feet, hands held, they pace the last
of what is theirs. No need for speech,
They walk united by their past.

They pass, united by the walk
of other pairs of lovers, some
still young, engaged in lovers' talk,
not yet aware that love is dumb.

The tide goes out, the tide comes back,
as one and one and one retrace
their steps to hunt for what they lack
but never find. Their other face.

Broken quatrains of faltering feet
search for a time they cannot beat.

Moving Right Along

She travels incessantly —
flies to Paris …
Delhi, St Petersburg,
Marrakech;
this saves her from facing
the time she has left.
Vicarious living
replaces lost love;
she circles the planet
in active distress.
Beauty departed,
she substitutes grooming;
her wardrobe is tasteful
and slightly outré.
Her cats are in kennels;
she sends them small presents
or postcards depicting the Appian Way.
Sips coffee in Venice,
then watches the tennis
at Wimbledon
wearing dark glasses and hair.
Her heart isn't breaking,
she's simply been faking
an interest
since love lost her somewhere out there.

She finds her denouement
while watching a sunset —
stone dead in a cafe,
it's quite an improvement.

Her Gucci accessories
go to a charity.
All of her jewellery
goes to her cats.
She leaves city real estate
in perpetuity
to homeless animals,
also her hats.
Her angry relations
expected no better.
It's too late to vet her
or raise caveats.

A lonely young sculptor
who hoped for a token
is hurt and heart-broken.
He smashes her bust
and vows that from now on
he'll guard against women
and drinks himself silly
while cursing at lust.
In various places
her face is remembered
by waiters and strangers
to whom she was kind.

Her life wasn't blameless
but something elusive
was left by her fragrance.
An oddly refined
need for reclusive simplicity.
Trust, in all that was courteous
and well designed.

Daft

If I go daft before you, Dear,
please read to me and prop me up
to see the sea, and share a cup
of coffee, strong, and stay as near
as bearable before I gape
into white space and start to stink.
That's when to leave my side I think.
When I am just a dribbling shape.

I'll stay with you if you tip first,
and play the music you like most,
make strange bruschetta things, or toast.
I'll read you Wodehouse, quench your thirst.
I'll show you parrots, pour you wine,
watch Monty Python or Totò
as smiling you'll forget you know
a face that once you knew was mine.

If we go daft together we
will die like fools without a clue.
You won't help me, I won't help you.
We'll blunder independently,
we'll shut us out, or lock us in,
set us on fire, or lose ourselves
behind the supermarket shelves,
each imbecile the other's twin.

Articulated

The thought that leapt into my head
when I was told of nuclear war
was: All grasshoppers will be dead.

And then it was as if I saw
their jigsaw, zigzag, tensile limbs
Meccano-jointed, ready for

Olympic heights in leafy gyms.
Darwinian prodigies that spring
in arcs as freedom's metonyms

for absolutely anything
unfettered where the will finds ways
to levitate somehow, to cling

on any apex where its gaze
looks further to more distant peaks.
And so the seeker never stays,

but leaves the stage to one who speaks
for those articulations lost
to grounded military cliques

who hate, and hurl their one riposte:
annihilation, endless night,
to win the fight, despite the cost.

the art of the matter

Eternal Hope

*To A. D. Hope, the great Australian poet
(after his poem 'Australia', written in 1939,
when Aborigines were officially not there)*

How blind our Homer was, our national Hope
who resolutely had refused to see —
'Without songs, architecture, history' —
the soft dark dancers. Bigot, misanthrope?

Yet he was neither, locked into his tribe,
expecting stone cathedrals, unaware
that other kinds of human life were there,
more subtle than a poet could describe.

Our Homer must have found those people odd.
Their songs were gifts from birds and beasts, inspired
by closeness to the earth. They walked unshod.
Their art was *not* to mark the ground they trod,
but breathe the rhythm that the bush respired,
and live too close to feel apart from God.

Sightlines

(Lloyd Rees, Sydney painter)

Old architect and draftsman had in hand
and eye the stretch of light and line,
                              the taut,
the tight, the free, the deep. And so the grand
old man did not fear blindness as he sought
the elements that bound him to the earth.

Beneath his tennis shade he drew it in,
the saturated harbour that was worth
a thousand views of Venice.
                              With his thin
sun-weathered fingers he allowed his skill
to lead his fading eyes into the glare
forbidden by his doctor.
                              Only will
could re-ignite his vision. He stared down
the sun that splashed the water in his mind
and dived deep in the light he knew would drown
his reason with the sight that made him blind.

Rain from a Blue Sky

Like woodcut lines the golden rain slants down
through sunlight in a vision from Japan.
Blue sky with rain. Does English have a noun
for rain from skies so blue? A new köan.

One hand claps and a miracle appears:
white-gold, bright-green, clear-blue, wash clean your sight
with strokes like tears, or iridescent spears
cut by a master, lasered thin with light.

Hold it and print it on your inward eye.
Press firm to fix down rain on plain blue sky.

The Pigeons in the Square

Have reproduced with zeal,
Excreting everywhere.
Peace symbols leave their seal

In Rorschach blots of white.
Gigantic paintings lie
Exposed in broad daylight,

Open to the sky.
New layers grow each day,
Surprising morning eyes.

In vain the cleaners spray—
Nature wins the prize.
Hot action painters splash,

Hurl, drizzle, drop and drip.
Raking in the cash
Since what they paint is hip.

Queer how our eyes deceive.
Upstairs a Pollock draws
Art lovers, who believe
Realism bores—
Except for the naive.

To Franz Schubert (1797–1828)

Nacht und Träume

Some songs sing themselves, and you,
deep night song, pull the singer in
with sombre rocking chords, down to
that place you call "stilled hearts of men".
A quiet note, insidious,
without a quiver draws me on—
indolent, melodious,
a dark, hypnotic, moonlit song.
Frail composer, so soon dead.
Some sense of doom combined with peace
and fatalism spun this thread,
as though it led to your release.
But dreams continue after death,
exhaled upon a singer's breath.

Antal Szalai's Gypsy Band in an Australian Country Town

The country concert hall is full
of old Hungarians who've come
from miles away to hear the thrill
of tarogato, cimbalom,
but most of all—the violin.
And what a violin! They say
that after he had heard him play
Yehudi Menuhin embraced him,
so deeply had Szalai impressed him.
When they start there's such a shock:
as though the world had run amok
sound rips around the walls and hits
the ceiling, strikes the metal parts
of doors and watches, and the hearts
of sleepers who have come to life,
and young again, accept the knife
of youth and pain; the lightning bursts
in every space and now it's Liszt's
transfiguration, Gypsy grief
and desperation, time the thief,
it weeps then changes with a bang,
to pure delight as high notes hang
above the hall so high they hurt
with panpipes conjuring a bird;
they're old, this audience, and know
that this is love, the silent bow
that holds suspended all they are
then lets them down through sunlit air;
the gypsy and the bird are free
like them, they leave him thankfully

in songs and dances, out the door
to Queensland which they never saw
the way they see it now, with strings
to all the loved remembered things.

Celebrity Recital

If she was fat, well what of that?
Her E in alt could knock 'em flat.
She had charisma of a sort
and treated opera like a sport.
A heavyweight, she hit the scales
with all she had. The nightingales
in Berkeley Square were wimps compared
with her excesses. When she bared
her flesh in dresses cut like tents
her old admirers lost all sense.
They pelted blossoms at the diva,
in a mad collective fever.
Heaving cleavage, she rewarded
those who had her voice recorded.
More, Encore, Bis, Bis, they shouted.
Even critics sometimes doubted
what their head had contradicted:
were their judgements too restricted?
When she shyly gave an encore
everywhere there was an uproar.
'Now I sing a lullaby'
and not a single eye was dry.
Her wig was hot, her bunion hurt,
the seam was going on her skirt.
The show completed, withers wrung,
no-one could say she hadn't sung.

empirical judgments

Out Loud

What if a poet wrote just for sounds
unsaid but felt? What then? What if
no reading could add to the rise and fall
and saying out loud made fluid stiff?
Say sonics exceeded linguistic bounds
and only the head but not the lips
permitted the thing to work at all?
A voice may stagger behind a mind
that dances along on its fingertips,
since poems like love, are often blind
and Braille must fail any penmanship.
A poem read on the printed page
may shimmer and blaze with a rat-tat-tat,
but when performed upon a stage
the poem may shrivel and fall down flat.

To a Dying Rat

Rat, I did not lay the bait
that's brought you to this parlous state.
Your dulling eyes encounter mine
and I recall the famous line:
'Wee, sleekit, cowrin', tim'rous beastie'
and grieve with Burns, but then at least he
saved the mouse, whereas I watch
your death old rat, and cannot scotch
the human habits that determine
which are pets and which are vermin.

Despite

Despite your lapses of good taste,
your vanity and need for praise,
despite the thickness of your waist,
your gluttonous, material gaze,
despite your kittenish pretence
of 'girlie talk' at sixty-five,
your total lack of common sense,
your drunken binges, know that I've
abstained from showing how I feel
and smiled although I want to kill
you for the way you try to steal
my husband. Though you make me ill
I'll never let you know that I
won't hold a party when you die.

light at the end

Seen From Above

driving to Brisbane

Seen from above, our little yellow car
winding up hilly country gravel roads,
shiny and silly among rough trucks with loads,
must appear inappropriate and bizarre.
Is it, perhaps, the very thing we are?

Lovely, the blend of dust and leaf and wood,
balanced by birdsong and the tractor's roar;
action and stillness as our spirits soar,
racing the sun before dark shadows could.
Everything, Pangloss said, is for our good.

Blinded by sunset, tree-flashed, into night,
darkness and moonlight up the motorway,
silvered into the city near the bay
sparkling like fireflies flirting with our sight,
over the great black river framed by light.

Seen from above we blend and disappear.
So many stories. Listen, the laughter bursts,
and ricochets off stone walls. Each spirit thirsts
after the gift of somewhere free from fear.
Seen from above this fragile life is dear.

Powerless

An accidental night of stars
stretched everywhere across the sky.
Dark houses, cinemas and bars
extruded people asking why?
No haze now from electric light
obscured the childhood memories
of mystery that pricked the night
when human light was less than these.
The stars swept further than the sea,
their diapason strong to some
who felt a pulse that used to be
and shivered, humble, overcome.
Now only when machines break down
do we perceive the ancient shape
inside our minds. This coastal town
is shocked. Struck dumb. We stand and gape.

Butterflies

Today is a day of butterflies but how can I
write of such things for people in cities, caught
in human closeness. If I ever thought
that they could care that all the air of my
garden is crowded with light uplifting
colour and whiteness, wafting, shifting,
I only need to remember the traffic clanking
and think of the feet on the pavement spanking
clipping and shuffling, and voices merging,
decibels surging and iron screeching,
thumping and thudding and Muzak reaching
into the buildings where lovers are lunching,
people are buying and selling, munching
something in paper, and rushing and crossing,
pissing and bossing and talking and meeting:
I and my butterflies are retreating.
Once I was part of the clutter and clatter.
I mixed and I struggled and joined the chatter
and oh, how I loved it, the smells and the fashions,
the colour and movement, the joy and passion.
Here with the butterflies in my garden
I bless the living and ask their pardon.

About the Author

Janet Kenny was a painter and concert singer in New Zealand until she went to the United Kingdom. There she sang in opera professionally until she retired early because of health problems.

She moved to Australia, where she was active in the disarmament and anti-nuclear movement in Sydney. She jointly edited, compiled and wrote *Beyond Chernobyl*, published by Envirobook in 1993. She now lives in Queensland with her husband of many years.

Her poems have been published in printed and online journals, including *Avatar, The Chimaera, Folly, 14 x 14, Iambs & Trochees, The Literary Review, Mi Poesias, The New Formalist, The Raintown Review, The Shit Creek Review, Snakeskin, Soundzine, The Susquehanna Quarterly* and *Umbrella*. Her work is in the collections *The Book of Hope* and *Filled With Breath: 30 sonnets by 30 poets*. She has received three Pushcart nominations.

www.ingramcontent.com/pod-product-compliance
Lightning Source LLC
LaVergne TN
LVHW020100090426
835510LV00040B/2749